Grandfather Owl

Written by Eun-hee Na
Illustrated by Sook-gyeong Kim
Edited by Joy Cowley

There is a sad song in the forest.
Boo-hoo! Boo-hoo! Boo-hoo!
It comes from a big oak tree
where a grandfather owl cries
because he is very lonely.

Spring comes to the forest.
The ice in rivers has melted
and there are green shoots
on the branches of the trees.
Still the grandfather owl cries,
Boo-hoo! Boo-hoo! Boo-hoo!

When the lilacs are in flower,
the grandfather owl hears a new noise.
Branches are rustling in his oak tree!
He opens one eye. And what does he see?
Two flying squirrels have moved into a hole
in the tree, and they've made a nest.

A few days later,
three flying squirrels are born.
One, two, three, cute little babies!
The grandfather owl pretends not to see,
but he is watching those baby squirrels,
with squinty loving eyes.

Then two nightingales sing in the tree.
The couple have made a nest of twigs
and there are two nightingale babies.

One, two! The grandfather owl counts
the baby nightingales in the nest.
He adds the three baby flying squirrels.
One, two, three, four, five babies!

The grandfather owl smiles
a secret, feathery smile.

> Counting up the baby animals is doing addition.
> 3 baby flying squirrels + 2 baby nightingales = 5 baby animals
> $3 + 2 = 5$

Three baby flying squirrels
and two baby nightingales
play in the oak tree branches.

The grandfather owl sleeps in the day
but he tries to stay awake to see
the five happy babies.

Very soon, there are five more babies.
One, two, three, four, five racoons!
The grandfather owl counts them
and adds them to the nightingale babies
and the flying squirrel babies.

One, two, three little flying squirrels.
One, two little nightingales.
One, two, three, four, five racoons.
That is one, two, three, four, five,
six, seven, eight, nine, ten babies!

3 baby flying squirrels + 2 baby nightingales + 5 baby racoons = 10 baby animals
3 + 2 + 5 = 10

One day there is a big rainstorm.
The racoon's burrow is destroyed
and the racoon babies have to find
a new home in the forest.

The grandfather owl is sad.
If five is taken away from ten,
then only five is left.

Doing subtraction is taking away parts from the whole.
10 baby animals − 5 baby racoons = 5 baby animals
10 - 5 = 5

A badger family moves into the burrow
that has been left by the racoons.
The badger couple have three babies.

The grandfather owl is happy again.
He counts the three baby badgers!
Three added onto five is eight.
Eight isn't as many as ten,
but it is still a good number.

5 baby animals + 3 baby badgers = 8 baby animals
5 + 3 = 8

A few days later,
a terrible thing happens.
A weasel comes to the oak tree
while the parents are away.

The weasel runs into the forest
with a baby flying squirrel
and a baby nightingale
in its mouth.

8 baby animals - 2 baby animals (1 baby flying squirrel and 1 baby nightingale) = 6 baby animals
8 - 2 = 6

The grandfather owl blames himself
because he was asleep when it happened.
He cries, "Boo-hoo! It is all my fault!"
and he counts the babies that are left.
Two away from eight leaves six.
One, two, three, four, five, six.

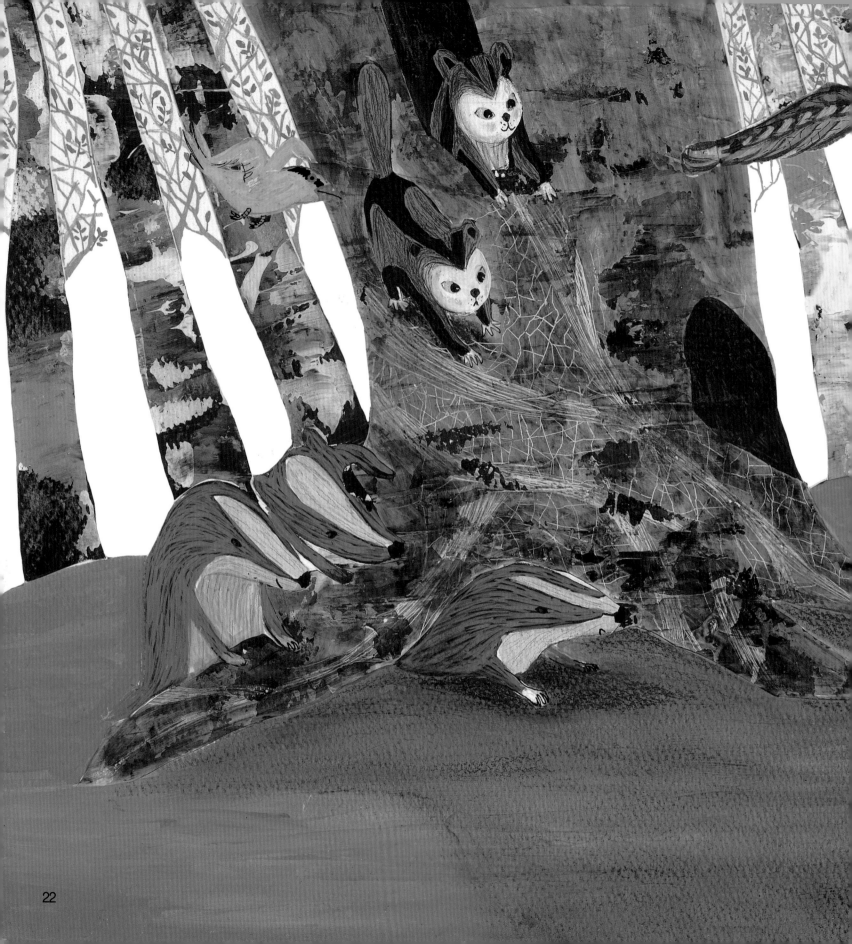

A few days later,
the oak tree has some new visitors.
Four baby red squirrels arrive
to make the tree their home.

The grandfather owl is delighted.
One, two, three, four, he counts.
Four added onto six is ten!
Once more, there are ten babies!

6 baby animals + 4 baby red squirrels = 10 baby animals
6 + 4 = 10

Time goes by, the babies grow,
and summer changes to autumn.
When cold winds blow in the forest,
the nightingales fly to a warm land
and the flying squirrels find a place
where they can sleep all winter.

"Three babies have left," says the owl.
"Now I have only seven."

10 baby animals - 3 baby animals (2 baby flying squirrels and 1 baby nightingale) = 7 baby animals
10 - 3 = 7

Next to go are the four red squirrels.
The forest becomes very quiet.
The owl is sad. "Four more have left!
Four gone from seven is three.
Soon the three badgers will go too
and then I'll have no one."

7 baby animals - 4 baby red squirrels = 3 baby animals
$7 - 4 = 3$

As the three badgers wave goodbye,
they call to the grandfather owl.
"We'll come again next spring
with the flying squirrels and the racoons
and the red squirrels and the nightingales.
We'll all be back and you will have
lots of babies in your tree."

3 baby badgers - 3 baby badgers = 0
3 - 3 = 0

The owl falls into a deep sleep
and has happy dreams of spring
when all the grown-up babies
will return with their babies.

There is only one problem.
He doesn't know if he will
be able to count them all.

Grandfather Owl takes care of the babies. Count the animals!
When you add more, that is addition.
When you take some away, that is subtraction.

3 badgers and 4 red squirrels
make 7 baby animals altogether.

$3 + 4 = 7$

3 badgers and 4 red squirrels
and 2 racoons make 9 baby animals.

$3 + 4 + 2 = 9$

There are 9 animals altogether.
If 3 badgers go away,
there are only 6 baby animals left.

$$9 - 3 = 6$$

There are 6 red squirrels and racoons.
If 2 nightingales come,
there are 8 baby animals altogether.

$$6 + 2 = 8$$

There are 8 animals altogether,
4 red squirrels move away.
Only 4 baby animals are left.

$$8 - 4 = 4$$

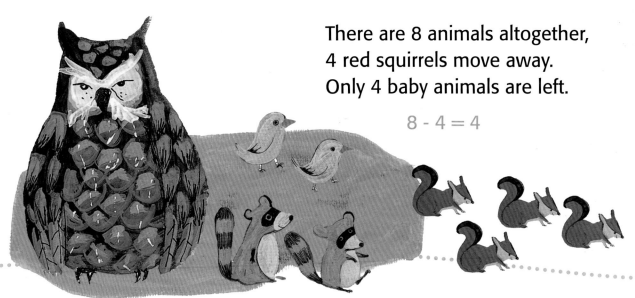

Oak Tree Playground

The grandfather owl has made hats for the baby animals.
Each hat has a coloured leaf.

1

There are 3 yellow-leafed hats
on one wing,
and 4 red-leafed hats
on the other wing.
How many hats are there altogether

2

Two nightingale babies wore
the red-leafed hats and then
flew away.
How many hats were left?

3

How many baby animals are playing hide and seek with the grandfather owl?

I found you! I found you!

4

The grandfather owl found two nightingales. How many baby animals are still hiding?

Answers: 1. 7 hats **2.** 5 hats **3.** 9 baby animals **4.** 7 baby animals

Original Korean text by Eun-hee Na
Illustrations by Sook-gyeong Kim
Korean edition © Yeowon Media Co., Ltd.

This English edition published by big & SMALL in 2015
by arrangement with Yeowon Media Co., Ltd.
English text edited by Joy Cowley
English edition © big & SMALL 2015

ISBN: 978-1-925234-13-8

Printed in Korea